Discovering Cabrillo

In this allegorical engraving the ship commander is holding an image of San Salvador, the Holy Savior.

Discovering Cabrillo

by Harry Kelsey

Liber Apertus Press
Saratoga, California
2017

Liber Apertus Press
P.O. Box 261
Saratoga, CA 95071 USA

www.liberapertus.com

ISBN 978-0-9785881-3-7

Published in the United States of America

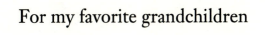

For my favorite grandchildren

Table of Contents

7

Illustrations

9

The Commander of the Armada

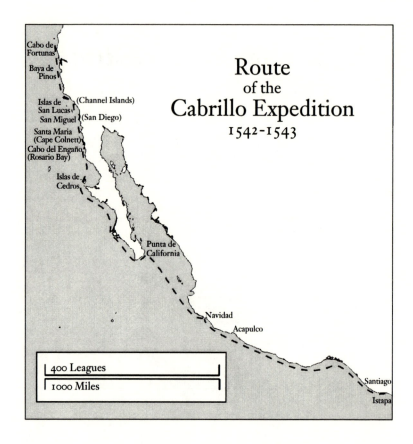

Route
of the
Cabrillo Expedition
1542-1543

Cabo de Fortunas
Baya de Pinos
Islas de San Lucas (Channel Islands)
San Miguel (San Diego)
Santa Maria (Cape Colnett)
Cabo del Engaño (Rosario Bay)
Islas de Cedros
Punta de California
Navidad
Acapulco
400 Leagues
1000 Miles
Santiago
Istapa

In Cabrillo's calculations a league was equivalent to about two and a half miles.

The Commander of the Armada

The year was 1543. The time, Christmas. Three Spanish ships were in the harbor of an island their commander had named San Salvador (known today as Santa Catalina) to honor the holy patron of his flagship. The *capitan-general* himself was on deck, watching as three or four sailors rowed a small boat ashore, carrying empty barrels to fill with drinking water. Coming to rest on a narrow, rocky beach, the men jumped out of the boat and began rolling their wooden casks uphill, where a spring flowed out of the rocks. Suddenly, half a dozen bowmen appeared from the underbrush and began to assault the Spaniards with stones and arrows. Their retreat cut off, the seamen took shelter behind the rocks and waited for their attackers to lose interest.

The men in the shore party were probably more annoyed than afraid. Their opponents were the same local people who had been friendly three months earlier. But it was summer then, when food was plentiful. Now the newcomers had out-stayed their welcome. The guests had become competitors, for winter was the season when food was scarce.

Determined to end these nuisance attacks, Captain Juan Rodríguez Cabrillo ordered a boatload of soldiers to row ashore, with the captain himself in command. Disaster struck just as the boat touched the beach. Before the men had even shipped their oars, the captain leapt from the boat, but the footing was treacherous. He slipped on the rocks, fell, and splintered his shinbone. The men were easily rescued, but the commander had a ghastly wound. Back on board, the surgeon made an attempt at treatment, but the wound quickly became morbid. Within a few days Juan Rodríguez Cabrillo was dead. He was buried on the island where he fell. The Spanish seamen had been calling the place *capitana*, which was a general name for a flagship. Now the island was renamed Capitana, because that was the place the *capitan-general* had died.

The origins of this great Spanish conquistador have been a matter of dispute. During the past century or so, several writers have said that Cabrillo was Portuguese, basing their claim on a remark by the Spanish chronicler Antonio de Herrera y Tordesillas. Writing more than half a century after the explorer's death, Herrera referred to him as Juan Rodríguez Cabrillo Portugues. Most historians now accept that this was an error.

Cabrillo's family and friends always insisted that he was from Spain. Members of his family swore this under oath, as did his friends. Most recently Dr. Wendy Kramer discovered documents in the Archivo General de Indias that establish the explorer's birthplace as Palma de Micer Gilio, a town on the Rio Guadalquivir about half way between Seville and Cordoba.

Juan Rodríguez Cabrillo de Aldana: "General Juan Rodríguez Cabrillo, my paternal great-grandfather, came to these parts from the kingdoms of Spain."

Regardless of his origins, very early in life Juan Rodríguez seems to have found himself in Seville, as nearly everyone did who sailed to the New World in those days. Juan Rodríguez may have come to the New World in the armada of Pedro de Arias that sailed from Seville in 1514. He served in Cuba and by 1520 was part of the army of Pánfilo de Narváez. Tough and self-reliant as a boy, Juan Rodríguez soon learned to shoot a crossbow, and he joined in the conquest of Mexico both as a soldier and a merchant adventurer. Along the way he learned to read, to write, to keep accounts, and to trade goods for a profit. He also acquired new military skills: how to ride a horse, and how to build and sail a ship.

In 1520 Rodríguez went to the mainland with Narváez, joined the army of Hernán Cortés, and served in the second attack on the Aztec capital, Tenochtitlán. The city was situated in the middle of a lake, and Cortés decided it was vulnerable to attack by water. Consequently, he sent troops to the mountains to cut timber and build a fleet. A story told

over and over again features Juan Rodríguez as commander
of a detachment sent to gather resin in the pine forests above
the city. Mixed with tallow, the resin became pitch, used for
waterproofing ships. With no animal fat to use for tallow,
the detachment is said to have used human fat from Indians
killed in battle. True or not, the story reflects the reputation
of Juan Rodríguez, a tough and resourceful conquistador,
with few or no inhibitions, determined to do whatever was
necessary for victory.

For the next decade Juan Rodríguez marched with the
Spanish armies through various parts of Mexico and Central
America, first with Francisco de Orozco, and then with Pedro
de Alvarado, commanding a squadron of crossbowmen. By
1532 he was settled in Santiago de Guatemala, with a generous grant of land, plus Indian laborers to do the work. One
of the richest men in the country, he controlled gold mines
and had ships sailing to trade with Spanish soldiers involved
in the conquest of the Inca empire.

During these years, Juan Rodríguez had an Indian wife
and several daughters. Perhaps this wife died, for in the fall
of 1532 he returned to Spain and married the daughter of
a prominent family of Seville. In due time Beatríz Sánchez
de Ortega gave him two sons. About this same time Juan
Rodríguez added Cabrillo to his name. It was probably a
nickname, but the meaning is not clear.

While all this was going on, several Spanish expeditions
entered the Pacific Ocean through the Straits of Magellan,
sailing for the Indies. Pedro de Alvarado conceived his own
daring plan to cross the Pacific from Mexico and begin to

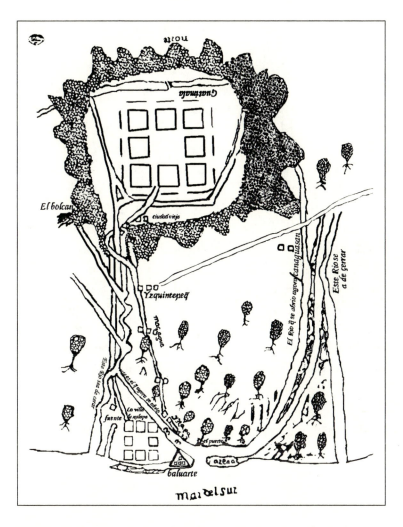

Istapa is at the bottom center of this late sixteenth century sketch. Santiago is at the top, surrounded by volcanoes.

trade with the Spice Islands and China. Under Alvarado's orders, Cabrillo built and assembled a fleet at the Guatemalan port of Istapa. Once the work was finished, Cabrillo joined the fleet as *almirante* or second in command, serving with his own ship, *San Salvador*. Alvarado died along the way, killed in battle with the Mixton Indians, and the viceroy of New Spain decided to split the fleet. Part of it was given to Ruy López de Villalobos, who was to sail across the Pacific and try to reach the Spice Islands. The remaining ships, *San Salvador*, a smaller ship named *Victoria*, and a launch called *San Miguel*, were reassigned to Cabrillo. He was to sail north, rounding the Pacific rim and meeting the fleet of Villalobos near "the Spice Islands and China." Along the way he was to look for the mouth of a river called Rio de Nuestra Señora, which was thought to flow from the Colorado river into the Pacific Ocean. In addition he was supposed to look for a good place to plant a colony. All of this was to be accomplished in an area that was unmapped and largely unknown.

The Coast of Lower California

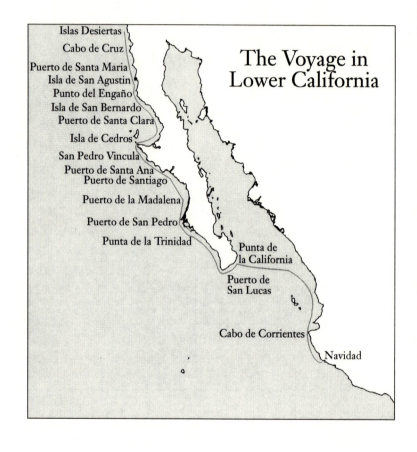

Islas Desiertas
Cabo de Cruz
Puerto de Santa Maria
Isla de San Agustin
Punto del Engaño
Isla de San Bernardo
Puerto de Santa Clara
Isla de Cedros
San Pedro Vincula
Puerto de Santa Ana
Puerto de Santiago
Puerto de la Madalena
Puerto de San Pedro
Punta de la Trinidad

The Voyage in
Lower California

Punta de
la California
Puerto de
San Lucas
Cabo de Corrientes
Navidad

The Coast of Lower California

With a treacherous southerly wind blowing across the bows, Juan Rodríguez Cabrillo led his fleet out of the harbor at Navidad, on the Mexican coast, at noon on Tuesday 27 June 1542. By 2 July the ships were within "sight of California," as the summary account of the expedition puts it. On Monday the third of July they anchored off the Punta de California. The name was applied a year earlier by Fray Antonio de Meno, referring to the discoveries of the Francisco de Ulloa expedition. Later that year Domingo del Castillo put the name on his map of the California peninsula. Very likely Ulloa's men used the word California as a joke. The popular Spanish novelist Garcí Ordoñez de Montalvo, had popularized the name in his story of the adventures of a certain knight named Esplandián. California, in Montalvo's account, was a place inhabited solely by women and ruled by a gorgeous queen, who allowed men on the island once each year or so for a ceremony of singular character. The island was "at the right hand of the Indies," and the ceremony was one aimed at continuing the race, in the usual way. The funny part of the story was that this barren and hostile coast and its inhabitants bore no resemblance to the beautiful women in the "earthly paradise" described by Montalvo.

Continuing north, but hugging the coast, Cabrillo and his ships visited all the islands and bays noted by the earlier explorers, finally passing the Cabo del Engaño (Rosario Bay) on 20 August. This was the place where Ulloa had turned back. From this point onward Cabrillo and his men were in uncharted waters. Two days later they stopped in a sheltered bay where there were several villages, whose inhabitants gave them a friendlier reception than any they had met previously. Cabrillo distributed some clothing and small gifts, and soon others came to lead his men to a spring of fresh water.

Later five other Indians appeared on the beach and asked to be taken out to see the ships. Their bodies were painted in

On the first part of his journey Cabrillo brought his armada north along the coast from Guatemala (lower right) to Navidad. He then sailed past Cabo de Corrientes and across the Mar Vermejo to California (just above the meridian). This map by Diego Gutiérrez is from 1562, the earliest printed map naming the California coast.

black and white to resemble the jackets and slashed doublets of Spaniards, decorations very similar to those seen by the traveler von Langsdorff at Mission San José two centuries later. These people said they had met bearded men who brought dogs and carried crossbows and swords and who looked just like the men on the ships. These men were some five days journey toward the interior. Almost certainly they had seen Ulloa and his men in 1539, but on the off chance that they were talking about Coronado, Cabrillo wrote a letter and asked the Indians to deliver it for him. Much the same story was repeated in other places. It seems to have been a common response by the local people, who wanted to give pleasing answers to the very pointed questions of their fearsome looking visitors, answers that would send them on their way as quickly as possible.

Leaving these pleasant people on Sunday morning 27 August, the sailors almost immediately sighted another large island. Since the chaplains of the fleet were Augustinians, they named the new place Isla de San Agustin, whose feast would occur the next day.

The country improved considerably from this point, as did the people. The manuscript report gives a great deal of detail about these Indians, perhaps because Juan Rodríguez Cabrillo spent a good deal of ink on his own description. They were tall and well built. Some wore deerskins and possibly leather sandals similar to those worn in Mexico. They carried bows and flint-tipped arrows. Continuing their journey for a week or so, the Spaniards stopped again for a few days, taking formal possession of the place and naming it after the

An Indian of ye Southermost parts of California
as Returning from Fishing & another on his Barkloo

Virgin Mary, whose birthday is celebrated on 8 September. The inhabitants of this village were sturdy and robust, though they wore no clothes. No pictures survive, but the descriptions match those of the people pictured in reports two centuries later. They carried bows and flint-tipped arrows and fished from small rafts. There were forty of them in all. These Indians were not afraid of the Spaniards, and though natives and visitors could not understand each other, they entertained the explorers with a feast of roasted agave and fish. It requires little imagination to see why the Spaniards stayed so long. This was not only the largest group of Indians the expedition had met along the California coast, it was also their first encounter with genuinely friendly and generous people.

From here onward the landscape changed. The sailors called it "a good country from the looks of things. There are

broad savannahs, and the vegetation is like that of Spain."
Some of the trees reminded them of ceibas or floss-silk trees,
"except the wood is hard." These may have been ash or syc-
amores, for ceibas are not part of the natural flora here. The
country northward was most attractive, with "very beautiful
valleys, groves of trees, and low, rolling countryside." On the
twenty-sixth and twenty-seventh of September they passed
the Coronado Islands, which they called Islas Desiertas. They
marked the latitude at thirty-four degrees, a bit more than
a degree and a half too high, but a good estimate, given the
difficulty of navigation with the instruments then available.
The mainland was "a fine land, by its appearance, with broad
valleys and with mountains farther inland." As more trees
appeared, the landscape in places was covered with dense
smoke. This resulted from the aboriginal practice of burning the woods and meadows each fall to increase the harvest
of acorns and grass seeds and improve the browse for deer,
rabbits, and other small game.

The Channel Islands

The names of Islands and villages are shown (below and left of the coat of arms) in this detail from the 1559 world map of Andrés Homem.

The Channel Islands

On 28 September the fleet reached "a sheltered port and a very good one, to which they gave the name San Miguel," whose feast would be celebrated the next day. This was the first landfall in the area that later came to be known as Alta or Upper California. The name given to the new port seems to have caused some grumbling among the crew members, for *San Miguel* was the smallest vessel in the fleet. The crews of the other ships evidently demanded similar honor, so the next important discoveries were named after the other two ships, *San Salvador* and *La Victoria*.

The port named for the smallest ship in the fleet was San Diego Bay, one of the largest and best on the west Coast. After anchoring at the entrance to the bay, a party went ashore and saw a few men, most of whom fled. Three others seem to have been more curious than afraid, and they stayed to receive some gifts. Perhaps the presents were a disappointment. That night, when several Spaniards went ashore to fish with a net, some of the Indians returned, armed with bows and arrows and shot three of them, inflicting minor wounds.

The next morning another shore party rowed up the bay in a boat, perhaps the *San Miguel*, sounding the depth of the water and looking for other natives. Spying two children on the beach, they landed, captured them, and brought them back to the fleet. They were talkative children, but try as they might, no one could understand the language, and signs were useless. Consequently, the commander gave the children some shirts, a very generous gift, and sent them back ashore.

The good treatment accorded the native children seems to have strengthened the resolve of the adults. Three of them came out to the ships on the following morning and managed a lengthy conversation in sign language. They reported that further inland there were bearded men dressed just like those on the ships, armed with crossbows and swords. "They made gestures with the right arm as though they were using lances, and they ran about as though they were riding horses." According to the Indians, the bearded men had killed many natives, and this was the reason they had fled in fear when Juan Rodríguez and his men first approached them.

Leaving port on Tuesday, 3 October, the armada sailed slowly up the coast, noting many interesting valleys, broad savannahs, high mountains a few miles inland, and a great pall of smoke that told them the area was heavily inhabited. After two days of this, they sailed out toward some islands that lay about seven leagues, or twenty miles offshore.

Reaching the nearest island on Saturday the seventh, they named it San Salvador, after the expedition's flagship. This is the island now called Santa Catalina. The second island (now named San Clemente) they called Victoria, after the third ship in the armada. They went ashore on the nearer one, San Salvador, and as the boat approached, a great crowd of armed Indians appeared. Shouting and gesticulating, the Indians made it clear that they wanted the strangers to come ashore. But the women suddenly fled, and for a time it seemed as though this might be a trap. Finally, the Indians put down their weapons, and eight or ten of them piled into a canoe and paddled boldy out to the ships.

As usual, the commander gave the visitors beads and other gifts that pleased them. A little later all went ashore, the best of friends. As the narrative has it: "They felt very secure, the Spaniards, the Indian women, and everyone." During this brief visit an old man came up to the visitors and said that he had heard reports of bearded men dressed like the Spaniards somewhere on the mainland.

There were probably two chaplains on the expedition. One of them was Fray Julián de Lezcano, who had taken his vows as an Augustinian just a few months before joining the armada. No doubt he said Mass here, and it was here or in San Miguel (San Diego) that Mass was first said in California.

Anxious to continue exploring the vastly improved coastline, Juan Rodríguez Cabrillo and his men made a hasty departure from the islands, and the next morning they were in San Pedro Bay. The burning chaparral raised such thick clouds of smoke that they named the place Baya de los Fumos (the Bay of Smokes) or Baya de los Fuegos (the Bay of Fires). Cabrillo called this place "a good port and a good land with many valleys and plains and wooded areas." A few Indians came out to visit them in a canoe and repeated the now familiar story that bearded men just like the Spaniards lived somewhere to the north. At a place they named Pueblo de las Canoas (the large village at Mugu Lagoon) canoeloads of people came out to visit the ships and talk to the men. By this time the explorers were almost bored by the repeated story of bearded Christians marching through the interior. Intrigued but doubtful, Cabrillo dispatched another letter in care of some Indians who said they were going in that direction.

Channel Islands and Villages on the Homem Map

Ancon de S. Migel	I. desierta
B. de los fuegos	I. de la uitoria
Costa blanca	I. de S. Salvador
p. de las canoas	
p. de Sardinas	I. de S. Lucas
p. de todos Santos	I. de palma
c. de galera	I. de la conception

For the next few days the expedition sailed along the channel that runs between the nearby islands and the mainland, an area known now as the Santa Barbara Channel, with a southern extension called the San Pedro Channel. The islands themselves are now named the Channel Islands. Cabrillo called them the Islas de San Lucas, after the Apostle Luke, because he took formal possession of the islands on the feast of St. Luke. A few days later he recognized that these islands can be subdivided into two groups. Those near Santa Barbara constituted one group of San Lucas Islands (present San Mi-

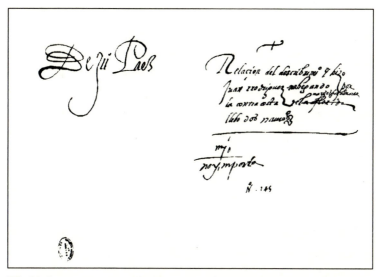

The Urdaneta manuscript had the name of Juan Paez de Castro on the cover sheet, a fact that has led some writers to name him as the author.

guel, Santa Rosa, Santa Cruz, and Anacapa). Those near San Pedro (present Santa Barbara, Santa Catalina, San Clemente, and San Nicolas) composed "the other islands of San Lucas."

The existing manuscript report of the expedition seems almost hopelessly confusing and repetitious regarding the locations of the villages on these islands and the mainland. The original record no longer exists, The report that has survived is a composite made by Andrés de Urdaneta, using accounts by several of the men who were on the expedition. Not all of them were on the same ship, nor did they visit the same places at the same times. And some were more successful than others in writing down the place names as the villagers called them out. Finally, Urdaneta was not completely successful in drawing the disparate accounts into a coherent narrative. As a result, what purports to be a list of village names in the narrative for 15 October is really a composite of several lists. The same holds true for a second list of that date, as well as a list dated 1 November, one following comments made for 3 January 1543, and one dated 12 January. For more than a century historians have disputed the exact locations of these places. But now with more information available than was previously the case, it is possible to clear up some of the confusion and to be reasonably certain about the whereabouts of the expedition.

On Friday the thirteenth of October the ships sailed further up the channel. Passing Quelqueme (Hueneme), Misinagua (Ventura), and Xuco (Rincón), they noticed the Anacapa Islands on the port side. From Indians who came out from the mainland they learned that these were uninhabited. The mainland was a country of broad savannahs, dotted with groves of trees. Passing the Rincón, where the lowlands of Carpinteria begin, they anchored on Saturday the fourteenth at Carpinteria Valley, a place that was both "very beautiful and filled with people, a level country with many trees." This proved to be one of the most pleasant spots on the voyage. Indians in canoes swarmed out to the ships with newly-caught fish to trade with the men of the armada. There were so many canoes at Xuco that it was like another Pueblo de las Canoas. As a result Spaniards called this place Pueblo de las Canoas as well, and then proceeded to give the same name to all the villages in the area, from Mugu to Xuco and beyond, a province that the Indians called Xucu. Xuco was the "primer pueblo de las canoas," or the chief town in that group. The Indians of the Pueblos de las Canoas became "great friends" of the Spaniards, at least for the time.

Sunday, 15 October, the armada continued its slow voyage up the heavily populated coast, passing Coloc (or Alloc, as it was also called), in the Carpinteria estuary, Xabagua (or Xagua) near present Montecito and, Cicacut (also called Ciucut, Xocotoc, and Yutum) near present Santa Barbara. At a village some four of five miles west of Goleta Point the local people brought them so many fresh sardines to trade that the Spaniards called the villages Los Pueblos de Sardinas. This was a different province with the additionally confusing name of Xexu, and Cicacut was the chief village.

On 16 October the fleet sailed further westward, passing Potoltuc (also called Partocac, Paltatre, and Paltocac), Anacbuc (also called Nacbuc), and Gwa, the latter two of which were located on small islets adjoining the mainland. They stopped for the night at two villages, now called Dos Pueblos, but then named Quanmu or Quiman.

On 18 October the ships of the armada neared Point Conception. Sailing west, as they were, the coastline appeared so long and low that it reminded the sailors of a galley, so they named it Cabo de Galera. As the northwest wind freshened, the ships found it impossible to sail around the cape. Coming about, they headed south toward the Channel Islands, landing and taking possession on the one now called San Miguel. In a singular failure of imagination they named this island La Posesión, just as they had done at San Salvador. All of the islands were called Las Islas de San Lucas, sometimes with a distinction between one group and the other.

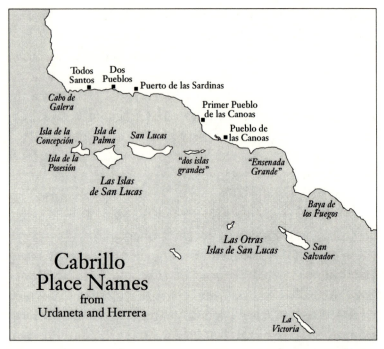

Cabrillo
Place Names
from
Urdaneta and Herrera

Todos Santos • Dos Pueblos • Puerto de las Sardinas
Cabo de Galera
Primer Pueblo de las Canoas
Pueblo de las Canoas
Isla de la Concepción   Isla de Palma   San Lucas   "dos islas grandes"   "Ensenada Grande"
Isla de la Posesión
Las Islas de San Lucas
Baya de los Fuegos
Las Otras Islas de San Lucas   San Salvador
La Victoria

The places visited and named by the Cabrillo expedition are recorded in the Urdaneta manuscript, the Homem world map, and the Herrera history.

At about this time Cabrillo made some effort to sort out the geography of the islands, most of which had been visited by one or another of his vessels while the rest of the armada made its way along the coast. Lázaro de Cárdenas, one of the seamen, testified later that Cabrillo took formal possession of every island, cape, and point visited by the flagship, "naming them and placing markers there." Cárdenas also confirmed a fact that was common knowledge among the men but somewhat muddled in the surviving manuscript:

that the principal island of San Lucas was called Capitana. This was the familiar name of the expedition's flagship, which was more formally called *San Salvador* and less formally called *Juan Rodríguez*. The island of Capitana (San Salvador and Juan Rodríguez) was also one of those called Posesión. This island was no doubt clearly marked on Cabrillo's maps and by the official marker Cabrillo and his men placed there in 1542. Thus, twenty-three years later, when Andrés de Urdaneta and Rodrigo de Espinosa made their pioneering voyage back across the Pacific from the Philippines, they had no doubt about its name or location. Before the voyage, when Friar Andrés first wrote about San Salvador, he said the island was in latitude "thirty-four degrees or more." This was the location Juan Rodríguez Cabrillo had given it, and this is the latitude it bears on surviving maps of the day, including the famous Homem planisphere. But when Urdaneta and Rodrigo de Espinosa arrived there in 1565, they calculated a more nearly correct latitude of thirty-three degrees and twenty-six minutes. Still, they recognized the island as San Salvador, a testimony to the quality of the records and charts brought back by the expedition of Juan Rodríguez Cabrillo.

On 1 November, the Feast of All Saints, the ships anchored at a village which they promptly renamed Todos Santos, though the natives called it Xexo,. The next day they sailed on to the Pueblos de Sardinas, anchoring at Cicacut, where they stayed for a few days taking on wood and water. The Indians at Cicacut were delighted to have the Spaniards back. The canoe masters came on board, dressed in their official capes and followed by Indian oarsmen. Indian musicians brought out their pipes and rattling reeds, and the sailors played Spanish bagpipes and tambourines. Dancing and feasting began. The elderly woman who was chief of this province stayed on board the flagship for the next two nights, along with a good many of her loyal subjects. These Indians were party-goers of great dedication, it would seem. Father Juan Crespí reported a similar celebration at the same place two centuries later. Juan Rodríguez and his men also loved a party, it seems, for they remained at the Pueblos de Sardinas until Monday, 6 November.

The captain general was impressed with the apparently abundant food supplies of this semi-agricultural society. During good years the wooded hillsides, lush grasslands, and coastal marshes furnished rich harvests of seeds and nuts, including acorns (from the *quercus agrifolia*), grass seeds, and cattail (*typha*) seeds used in preparing atole, pinole, and the mush cakes that Juan Rodríguez described as tamales, saying they were "good to eat." One of the seeds, probably the acorn, was "as large as maize and white," but maize itself was not grown or eaten there. As would be expected, the Indians ate fish, both cooked and raw, and maguey.

The local people painted and decorated themselves with beads and daggers of bone and stone and shell. Colorful feathers were stuck here and there in their coiffures, as style and taste dictated, but no detailed descriptions by the men of the expedition survive. Canoe owners and the leading chiefs wore capes of elk hide or bearskin, but most of the people wore nothing at all, a fact that brought no complaints from the men on the ships.

A woman was chief of the Pueblo de Canoas

With full stomachs and full water casks, the armada weighed anchor on Monday 6 November, sailing again toward Cabo de Galera. By 11 November they were running along the coast around Point Sal in the neighborhood of San Luis Obispo. With a stiff wind from the southwest and no sign of shelter along the coast they dared not attempt to anchor. Running before the wind, with only a small sail on their foremasts, the ships became separated in the rain and wind. The storm became fierce, and the *Victoria* lost all deck cargo and suffered much damage to masts and rigging. Led by the chaplain, the men on the San Salvador said special prayers to the Virgin, calling her Our Lady of the Rosary and the Blessed Mother of Piety. More frightened than at any other time on the voyage, they vowed to make a pilgrimage to her shrine if she would return them home safely.

The *San Salvador* had run out to sea, in order to avoid being driven onto the rocky shore. As the fury of the storm subsided, the vessel began to make its way back to shore. The sea remained high and the wind strong, and soon the men sighted Point Reyes, where the pilot measured the sun's position with an astrolabe and called the latitude forty degrees. They named the place Cabo de Pinos because of the great stands of Douglas fir and other evergreens that covered the hillsides. Confused by the hills beyond the inlet, the lookouts missed the entrance to San Francisco Bay, which everyone else did as well for the next two centuries and more. Instead, the ship rounded the point and sailed up the coast for another thirty-five or forty miles to the Russian River. Here the commander ordered the pilot to turn back.

South of the Cabo de Pinos the mountains (Santa Cruz) were covered with snow, evidently from a fresh storm the night of the fourteenth. The weather was so cold the seamen could scarcely man the sails. Then, on the morning of the fifteenth, they suddenly came upon the other ships lying at anchor. One, perhaps *San Miguel*, was leaking badly, and both crews were exhausted and half frozen. Continuing south, on November 16 the fleet entered the great harbor they had missed in the storm, now called Monterey Bay. Here as elsewhere they failed to find the great river. In fact, the surf was so high the boats could not even be sent ashore for wood and water. Instead, the ships cast anchor in forty-five fathoms. The captain general named the place Baya de los Pinos, computed the latitude at a bit more than thirty-nine degrees, and took formal possession in the name of the king of Spain and the viceroy of Mexico, as he had done at all the other capes and points and bays he discovered and named.

The leaky vessel stayed at anchor for another day, making hasty repairs, while the *San Salvador* beat about the bay looking for the river. The following day, Saturday, 18 October, the fleet sailed on south looking for a safer anchorage. Cypress Point was covered with snow, so the men called it Cabo de Nieve. The northwest wind cleared away the clouds, so they measured the altitude of the sun and computed the latitude at thirty-eight degrees and forty minutes, about two degrees too high.

The mountainous coastline south of Monterey Bay was covered with a blanket of snow, which lay so thick on the trees and cliffs that the men called the mountains the Sierras Nevadas, or the Snowy Mountains. The kind of snowy winter of these years is totally unknown in central and southern California today, but it was the prevailing weather pattern in the sixteenth century. This was the middle part of a cool-moist weather cycle that began about 1370, reached an extreme in 1770, and finally changed to the present warm-dry trend about 1860.

The high, rugged mountains along the coast were an imposing sight, covered with snow and ice. Sailing close to shore, as the narrative says they did, the shivering sailors thought the cliffs "were about to fall on the ships." Why they clung so close to the cliffs is still something of a mystery, for there was a heavy swell with breakers crashing on offshore reefs, and still no place to anchor. South of Cabo de Martín they again noticed signs of Indian settlements, but the high wind and heavy seas kept them headed for the islands.

The voyage ended on Thursday, 23 November 1542. Since there were two islands in the group called Posesión, the narrative explained that the armada arrived "at the Islands of San Lucas, at one of those called Posesión." This was doubtless the one now called San Miguel Island, where there is a good harbor, though a small one with a narrow entrance. The fragata *San Miguel* was by this time leaking so badly that the sailors on board thought it would sink at any time. They quickly hauled the small vessel ashore and began to recaulk the hull and repair the sprung planking. Their refuge, called Cuyler's Harbor, opens to the north, and the heavy swells that accompany the northwest winds make it a treacherous anchorage for much of the year. The other ships probably did not remain there for long, but sought shelter in the other islands.

The Coast of Upper California

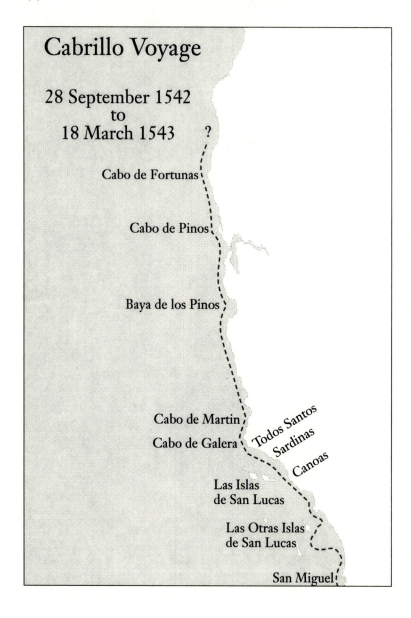

Cabrillo Voyage

28 September 1542
to
18 March 1543   ?

Cabo de Fortunas

Cabo de Pinos

Baya de los Pinos

Cabo de Martin
Cabo de Galera
Todos Santos
Sardinas
Canoas

Las Islas
de San Lucas

Las Otras Islas
de San Lucas

San Miguel

The Coast of Upper California

It is difficult to make much sense of the lists of islands and village names in this part of the narrative. The Homem map of the world, which dates from 1559 and was drawn from official reports, shows that the island now called San Miguel was then named Isla de la Concepción. No doubt this name was applied on the feast of the Immaculate Conception, 8 December, while the ships were sheltering there after the trip along the northern coast. Another island, called Limu in the narrative, is said to contain eight towns (though ten names are given). Moreover, it is a close neighbor to the islands of Ciquimuymu (or Posesión) and Nicalque. Linguistic evidence supports the conclusion that Nicalque is the one now called Santa Rosa Island. Another island, mentioned earlier in the narrative as San Lucas, is pretty clearly the one now called Santa Cruz Island. Limu is the one now called Santa Catalina, the island that sailors Lázaro de Cárdenas and Francisco de Vargas referred to as "la isla Capitana." They called it the most important island discovered on the expedition and the headquarters for all the fleet.

Here it was that the fleet wintered, according to Vargas and Cárdenas. The Indians who lived there quickly tired of the Spaniards and began a series of running battles with them. Vargas recalled that "all the time the armada was in the Isla Capitana the Indians there never stopped fighting us." On Christmas Eve or thereabouts the captain sent a party ashore for water, and the Indians attacked. The soldiers, outnumbered and sorely pressed, called out to the ship for help. Juan Rodríguez Cabrillo himself determined to rescue them, quickly gathered a relief party and rowed ashore in one of the launches. "As he began to jump out of the boat," said Vargas, "one foot struck a rocky ledge, and he splintered a shinbone." Somehow dragging himself ashore, the captain general refused to leave the island until all of his men were rescued.

There is some conflicting evidence about the nature of the injury. The younger Juan Rodríguez Cabrillo said in 1560 that his father had a broken leg, and Lázaro de Cárdenas verified this. But the manuscript narrative of the expedition says, "He broke an arm close to the shoulder." In a fall such as this, it is certainly possible that he broke both his arm and his leg. Vargas, however, insists that the injury was a shattered shinbone. "The witness knows this," said Vargas, "because he was right there." Juan León, a notary who took testimony from the survivors of the expedition in 1543 also took the testimony in 1560, and he saw no reason to question either account. Juan Rodríguez Cabrillo was taken back aboard ship, where the surgeon tried to treat the wound. However, the injury could not be helped with the medical knowledge then available. The wound quickly turned morbid. Knowing death was near, Juan Rodríguez called in his chief pilot to hand over command of the armada. He then proceeded to put his papers in the best order possible, though he was not able to summon enough strength to complete that part of his account that recorded the voyage north of the Channel Islands. This section of the narrative remains singularly lacking in detail, having none of the enlightening comments that enliven the earlier pages.

Unable to complete the voyage himself, Juan Rodríguez charged Bartolomé Ferrer with responsibility for doing so and further ordered him to make a complete report to the viceroy. Once this was done, according to Cárdenas, "He called Captain Ferrer and gave him command as captain general of the armada, by the authority of the royal commission that he held." Juan Rodríguez Cabrillo died on 3 January 1543, and

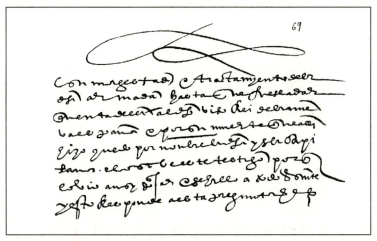

Cardenas: "y por su muerte que alli hizo quedo por nombre la dicha ysla capitana" (middle of line four to beginning of line six).

was buried on the island Capitana. "Because he died here," said Cárdenas, "the island retained the name Capitana."

The fleet remained in the island until 19 January, then headed for the mainland in search of supplies for a renewed journey to the northwest. However, violent winds swept the channel and kept the ships from making their way ashore. The ships were forced to return to Capitana, sailing around the islands for several days in search of shelter. During this time they anchored in the lee of the island they called San Lucas (Santa Cruz), but the stormy seas forced them to cut their cables and make a hasty exit. They returned at the end of the month to retrieve the anchors, took on a few more barrels of water, then tried again to sail to the mainland villages. El Puerto de Sardinas, which had seemed such a rich village in the summer, now had few inhabitants and no extra food. The ships came away with only a small boatload of firewood and nothing else.

Deciding to take advantage of the strong northeast wind, the fleet sailed southwest from the island of Capitana. Here the pilots reported finding "six islands, some large and some small." As Henry Wagner says, it is useless to try to guess which islands these might have been. Nor is it easy to guess where or why they went toward the southwest for the next few days.

On Thursday, 22 February, "they made another turn toward land in order to go in search of the Cabo de Pinos, with a south-southwest wind that lasted for three days, each day getting stronger. The following Sunday at daybreak they caught sight of the Cabo de Pinos." This was near to

A ship of about 1541 from the "Roteiro of Dom Johann de Castro."

the most northerly point they had reached on the previous voyage. Sailing farther north, they reached Point Arena on 26 February, and called it Cabo de Fortunas for St. Fortunatus, whose feast it was. Then, as the wind continued to build, they sailed on northward until they thought they were in latitude of 43 or 44 degrees, though they were probably some two degrees farther south.

On 28 February, the storm increased in intensity, with huge waves breaking over the ships, so that the two ships

without sterncastles, *San Miguel* and *Victoria*, were nearly
swamped. In these straits, the sailors made new vows to the
Virgin – this time to Our Lady of Guadalupe—promising
another pilgrimage if they were saved from the storm. Since
it was most unlikely that any of the sailors would ever return
to Spain for the pilgrimage, their prayer must have been to
the Virgin venerated at Guadalupe near Mexico City. If so,
this is one of the earliest recorded accounts of veneration of
the Mexican Virgin.

As though in answer to their prayers, the wind shifted to the
north, and the ships were able to begin running back toward
their island haven. The seas remained high, and the waves
broke over the bows with crashing blows, "and passed over
them as though over a rock." Again they asked the Lord and
his Blessed Mother for a miraculous change in weather, and
again they thought they received an answer to their prayers.

They had not found the river they sought, "though it
seemed to them that there was much evidence of a river," in
the form of logs and other debris. The storm had damaged
their remaining stores, and the seamen were unable to continue fighting the winds. They turned back once more. For
the weakened survivors of many arduous months, the return
voyage would tap the last of their resources.

The Voyage Home

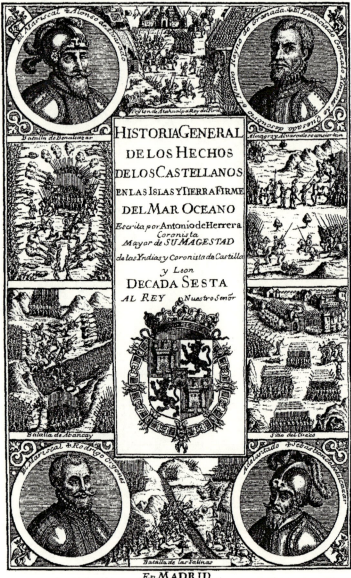

The Voyage Home

The fleet ran into rough weather again around the Channel Islands, again the ships became separated, and again each ship's crew thought the other ships were lost. However, the *San Salvador* took time to stop at the Pueblo de las Canoas, where four Indians were taken on board, and at San Miguel where two Indian boys were captured, all of whom to be trained as interpreters for a possible return voyage. If they had failed to comprehend the languages of the Indians, they had at least learned that trained interpreters could be very useful in dealing with the increasingly short-tempered Indians of California.

One of the ships (it may have been *La Victoria*) tried to run into the harbor at Capitana (Santa Catalina), scraped across the reef, and was very nearly lost. The vow to the Virgin this time was that the men would go to church stripped of all finery, if she would save them. Again the storm passed, but the ships remained separated. On Palm Sunday, 18 March 1543, *La Victoria* was apparently in the harbor at one of the northern Islas de San Lucas. Since this island had not yet been named, they decided to call it Las Palmas. Then they headed for home. That very same day, *San Salvador* departed from the harbor at San Miguel, the crew still uncertain what had happened to *La Victoria*.

Continuing south, all the ships of the armada were finally reunited off Cedros Island. Several men had died on the journey, from battle wounds or illness or hunger. The ships were battered and leaking. Supplies were nearly exhausted. Ferrer gave the orders to sail on to Navidad, where they arrived on Saturday, 14 April 1543, nearly nine months after embarking.

Mendoza's pleasure at their return was tempered by the news that the commander, Juan Rodríguez Cabrillo, had died and several other men as well. Moreover, the expedition failed to reach the Spice Islands or China, did not locate the Río de Nuestra Señora, and had no word of the Villalobos expedition. All the money, the supplies, the ships, the men had been wasted in a fruitless effort to find new riches. The Royal Audiencia demanded to know what had happened. Mendoza sent the notary Juan León to Navidad to question the survivors and record their accounts of the disastrous voyage. Four or five of these records were then summarized by Friar Andrés de Urdaneta and sent to the Viceroy. This manuscript now rests in the Archivo de Indias in Seville, the only such account of the journey to survive. From time to time it was consulted by the royal chroniclers and geographers Alonso de Santa Cruz, Juan Paez de Castro, Andrés García de Cespedes, Sancho Gutiérrez, and Antonio de Herrera y Tordesillas, several of whom put their signatures on the document to show they had read it. Urdaneta later used the

The first page of the Urdaneta manuscript has the signature of Juan Paez de Castro and Andrés García de Cespedes at the top, along with marginal notes by others.

records for another voyage across the Pacific and back, but that is another story.

With the survivors gathered in Navidad, Mendoza decided to keep the men assembled for a possible attempt to rescue Villalobos, from whom he had heard not a word. In order to keep them occupied, he refitted all three ships or took three others just like them and sent them off to Peru with horses and supplies to sell to the Spaniards there. Few of the men and none of the ships ever returned.

A similar fate befell those who went with Villalobos, and that commander also perished before his expedition was completed. Some years later the Dominican scholar Remesal wrote the epitaph for the great armada built by Juan Rodríguez Cabrillo: "The entire fleet perished, some eaten by shipworms, others scattered to different ports in disorder, because the adelantado had died."

The Sources

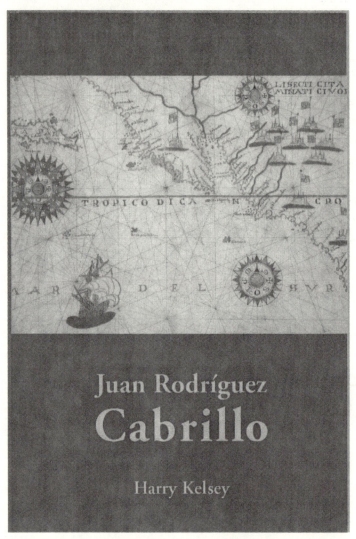

The author's full biography of Cabrillo was first published in 1986 by the Huntington Library; new edition available in 2018 from Liber Apertus Press.

The Sources

Readers who want a more detailed account should consult the author's biography of Juan Rodríguez Cabrillo, published by the Huntington Library. Copies are available in second-hand bookstores and many local libraries. A new edition will be published in 2018 by Liber Apertus Press (www.liberapertus.com).

The manuscript account of the journey prepared by Andrés de Urdaneta is in the Seccion de Patronato Real, legajo 20, in the Archivo General de Indias (A.G.I.), Seville, Spain. A translation apparently made by the American scholar Irene Wright can be found in Henry R. Wagner's book, Spanish Voyages to the Northwest Coast of America in the Sixteenth Century (San Francisco: California Historical Society, 1929). While this work is long out of print, a facsimile edition was published by Nico Israel in Amsterdam in 1966, and many libraries have copies of one edition or the other. The appendix to this work includes a good photostatic copy of the original manuscript.

Various manuscript copies of the sworn declarations by Francisco de Vargas and Lázaro de Cárdenas and other

friends, relatives and associates of Cabrillo are in the A.G.I.
(Justicia 280, Justicia 290, Guatemala 215, and Patronato 87).
Other copies are in the Archivo General de Centro America
(A.G.C.A.), Guatemala City (A.3.2, legajo 1539, expediente
22.569; A.1.29, leg. 2033, exp. 14084).

Recently an Augustinian scholar has published a brief
but well documented biography of Fray Julián de Lezcano,
one of the chaplains of the expedition. The author is Karl
A. Gersbach, and the work, "Fray Julian Lezcano, O.S.A.,
Member of the Cabrillo Expedition along the California
Coast 1542-1543," *Analecta Augustiniana* (2002), 65:71-90.
The journal may seem somewhat obscure, but the article is
packed with interesting information about the Augustinians
and their roles in early Spanish exploration. Most libraries
should be able to get copies on interlibrary loan.

For those who want to retrace the route of Cabrillo, the best
geographical analysis of the journey is that done by George
Davidson in the *Annual Report of the U.S. Coast and Geodetic
Survey for 1886*. His conclusions can be found in Appendix VII
(Washington: G.P.O. 1887), 155-253. The report is probably
available in most major libraries.

New information about Cabrillo's origins can be found
in a journal article by Dr. Wendy Kramer, "Juan Rodríguez
Cabrillo, Citizen of Guatemala and Native of Palma del Rio:
New Sources from the Sixteenth Century," *The Journal of San
Diego History*, Vol. 62, Summer/Fall 2016, 217-248.

Pictures and Maps

Cover: Braun & Hogenberg, *Civitates Orbis Terrarum* (Cologne: 1618).

Frontispiece: Copy (reversed) of an engraving from Jan van der Straet, *Americae Retectio*.

Page 15: A. G. I., Patronato 37, fol. 36v.

Page 46: A. G. I., Mapas Y Planos 518.

Page 22: Georg H. von Langsdorff, *Voyages and Travels in Various Parts of the World*. vol. II (London: Henry Colborn, 1814).

Page 23: Diego Gutiérrez, "Americae sive quartae orbis partes nova et exactissima descriptio" (Antwerp: Hieronymus Cock, 1562).

Page 24: George Shelvocke, *A Voyage Round the World* (1726).

Page 28: Andres Homem, "Universa ac navigabilis totius terrarum orbis descriptio," Ge.CC. 2719, Paris, Bibliothéque Nationale.

Page 33: "Relación del descubrimiᵒ q hizo Juan rrodriguez nabegando por la contra costa de la mar del sur al norte," A. G. I., Patronato 20, fol.1.

Page 38: George Shelvocke, *A Voyage Round the World* (1726).

Page 47: A. G. I., Justicia 290, fol. 68v.

Three-masted galleon of the late sixtenth century.

Page 49 and chapter openers: "Roteiro de Dom. Johann de Castro," British Museum Manuscript, Cotton Tiberius D. ix; published in Duarte Pacheco Pereira, *Esmeraldo de Situ Orbis*, trans. by Geo. H. T. Kimble (London: Hakluyt Society, 1937).

Page 52: Antonio de Herrera, *Historia general de los hechos de los Castellanos en las islas de Tierra Firme del Mar Oceano* (Madrid: N. Rodríguez Franco, 1726).

Page 55: "Relación del descubrimi° q hizo Juan rrodriguez nabegando por la contra costa de la mar del sur al norte," A. G. I., Patronato 20, fol.1v.

Page 62: Braun & Hogenberg, *Civitates Orbis Terrarum* (Cologne:1618).

Back cover: Reconstruction of Cabrillo's flagship, the *San Salvador*, which was launched in 2015. Photo by Jerry Soto, courtesy of the Maritime Museum of San Diego.

The route maps were made using Corel Draw 11 and Cartesia software. Other illustrations were retraced and otherwise enhanced with the same Corel software.

A broken metate found on San Miguel Island a century ago is often said to be the tombstone of Juan Rodríguez Cabrillo.

About the Author

Harry Kelsey is a historian and research scholar at the Huntington Library in San Marino, CA. His other books include:

*The First Circumnavigators:
    Unsung Heroes of the
    Age of Discovery*

*Philip of Spain, King of
    England: The Forgotten
    Sovereign*

*Sir John Hawkins: Queen
    Elizabeth's Slave Trader*

*Sir Francis Drake:
    The Queen's Pirate*

Juan Rodriguez Cabrillo

*Mission San Luis Rey:
    An Illustrated History*

*Mission San Juan Capistrano:
    A Pocket History*

*Mission San Luis Rey:
    A Pocket History*

CPSIA information can be obtained
at www.ICGtesting.com
Printed in the USA
FSOW02n0806260917
38972FS